Elaine,

Just thinking of you and wishing you lots of "little sunshine wishes"

Love You,

Linda

Little Wishes

Little Wishes
To Help You Feel
A Whole Lot Better

By Dean Walley
Illustrated by
Susan Morris

HALLMARK EDITIONS

Little Wishes

Here's a little book
      with lots
      of happy wishes in it,
just the kind
      of little wishes
      someone's wishing you
            this minute!

You're wished
  the happy feeling
  a child
    is sure to find
with a penny
  in his pocket
  and candy
    on his mind.

Hope you feel
  as warm and cozy
as you do
  when you wear mittens...

...and as dreamy-
drowsy-dozy
as a basketful
of kittens.

And may

every little problem

that comes raining down

on you...

...disappear
    amid the cheer
of sunny wishes
    shining through!

Here's a little wish
for happy times...
...a little wish
for laughter...

...and a wish
      for magic memories
      you can keep
         forever after.

Little wishes...
...like fireflies...
can brighten up
the night.

They can shine their way
into your heart
and make things
turn out right.

And no matter
   what the matter is
   you can laugh away
      your troubles...

...when little wishes
drift your way
like tiny,
shiny bubbles.

Every little wish
    that someone picks
        to send your way...

...is sure to bring you beauty
like a colorful bouquet.

And all the little notes of cheer
from those you're fondest of...

...will combine

    within your heart

    to fashion songs

    of joy and love.

*May each
   little wish twinkle
   in your heart
      just like a star...*

...They may seem small

    but you'll surely know

        how big they really are.

For wishes...
...just like candles...
can cast a cheery glow
that adds
a special meaning
to familiar things
we know.

*And every wish is meant
to bring you joy
in large and small ways...*

...and little though they are,
      they'll last
            today,
                  tomorrow,
                        always!